Excellence in Accelerated Learning:
Simple Ways to Train Yourself to Learn Faster, Sharpen your Memory and Become More Productive

By: Michael Holloway
ISBN: 9781094919508

Table of Contents

Introduction:

Ever get that feeling that your life is going nowhere?

If you have, then you will be relieved to know that you can redirect your destiny. Even better, it will cost you nothing but your time. ☐

In this guide, I will show you how caring for the 'self' can expand your horizons. Your mind and body really do need care and attention.

This guide suggests ways of improving your present lifestyle. It will show you the tools and information on how you can improve areas of your life, as well as uplift the sense of self.

It's not a complicated plan. It involves looking closely at your present lifestyle. Considering your dietary needs, basic exercise, and sleep patterns. These are all important factors that you need to challenge before you can embark upon changing your life around.

This is a guide that will encourage you to:

- Take care of the "self."

- Improve your memory skills.

- Teach you the importance of speed reading.

By learning to speed read you will learn to focus. It is the skill of "focus" that will lead to other accelerated learning. This, in turn, will improve your lifestyle and sense of who you are.

None of this will be easy. It takes self-discipline and confidence in yourself. Once you achieve it, you will go forward and benefit from your new lifestyle.

Let us help you to help your future.

Chapter 1: Self-regulation

Brain Power

The full potential of the human brain is still unknown. It's an organ that weighs on average around three pounds. Who would believe that it contains up to 100-billion interconnected neurons? Yet, this is how information travels around in our grey matter. It is a powerful organ that can:

- Process Information.

- Process complex images.

- Store Memory.

- Control body movements.

- Deal with toxins and flush them away.

- Keep our heart pumping and our lungs breathing.

And, these are only the basics.

Our perplexing brains are busily zapping away with electrical activity 24 hours a day. What's more, the brain continues to grow. It doesn't get any larger but develops more neurons as we actively learn. Researchers creating Artificial Intelligence (AI) showed that the human brain is 30-times more powerful than the world's fastest computer.

With such power going on inside your head, it does make you wonder what our real potential is.

Okay, back down to earth. In reality, we humans are very curious creatures. Mankind is constantly searching for answers to everything that comes their way. As a species, we have a deep routed curiosity to learn all we can throughout our life span. Psychologists label this as "Mastery." With such a capacity to absorb new information and adapt accordingly, you'd think all be equal to Einstein, yet, it's not that simple, is it? Learning takes effort on our part.

Knowledge doesn't just funnel itself into the brain and absorb into our neural network. We have to identify that new knowledge, and then we have to go through the grueling process of putting it there inside our heads so that we can learn from it. Learning new skills leads to a whole new thinking process of creativity. Who knows where this process ends, or can it be continuous throughout your whole life? Yes, it can.

Also as being inquisitive creatures, humans also possess a selfish yearning for praise and reward. Without rewards, we seem to lack motivation. In our industrialized world, we're taught to seek monetary rewards, believing this will lend us a better life. To some extent that is true, money can offer an easier existence. Being rich does not necessarily mean you are content with your lot in life. Excessive amounts of cash are no good if you're not a happy person. Imagine then, if you could combine happiness and have enough money to enjoy the better things of life. □

Can we create a set of circumstances to help us reach our ultimate goals in life?

That's where our clever brain comes in handy. The quicker we learn new skills, the sooner we gain those rewards. To learn at a faster pace though, we would need to craft the essential skill of focusing. This is where mindset comes into place, but what exactly is a healthy mindset?

Self-discipline

It is not an easy feat, to train your mind to focus. This takes time and commitment. Yet, just like training at the gym for a well-defined sculptured body, you can shape the way your mind thinks too. You can train your mind to focus by using the art of self-discipline.

It sounds too easy, doesn't it? Well, it's not! Self-discipline, or lack of it, can often be the downfall of many projects and personal ambitions.

A weight lifter knows that their body is capable of becoming stronger. The first rule they accept is that of self-discipline as they train. They must practice over and over as they perform difficult repetitive exercises. It is no easy task to build up strength, but that is the only way to reach their target. Healthy food is top of the list, and it takes hard work on their part to find a routine in life that works. Many are successful. Those are the ones who understand what they need to do to achieve their ultimate goal. Those who don't reach that goal have lost their way. They must settle for a lesser path, or go a different way altogether. □

The latter sounds like the option of the majority of the population. □

This takes us back to the wonderful organ called the brain. As the body can grow in strength, so too can the brain perform amazing feats.

We know the bodybuilder needs a routine to reach his/her target. That is no different from anyone who wishes to reach extraordinary levels. Many successful people have pushed their boundaries beyond normal limitations. □

How then does the average person do this?

This is where our journey begins.

Know Yourself

This is the only way you are going to drive yourself beyond your normal capability. Admit your faults, find your strengths and build up a routine that will follow a path to your ultimate goal.

This is where you must take a good look at who you are.

Ask yourself these basic questions:

- Do I eat healthy foods?

- Do I eat too much junk food?

- Do I get enough exercise?

- Do I read enough?

- How good is my concentration span?

How well do I sleep?

These questions cover some basic parts of your very existence. That is where you must begin and then build up the building blocks to success. Call it your preparation level. If you are that person who wishes to be successful, then prepare for the training, it can be done.

Chapter 2: Challenging Your Lifestyle Goals

In the previous chapter, I asked you to look at yourself, both internally and externally. To progress in life, you need to care for your body, mind, and soul. Only then can you achieve your life goals. If your diet consists of too much junk food, you most likely already know that type of diet is not good for you. It's time to take a close look at your present lifestyle and make some improvements. Ask yourself questions such as:☐

- Do you sleep well?

- How do you cope with stress?

- What is your exercise regime?

- How organized is your week's agenda?

Be honest in your answers because if you're not, you are only letting yourself down. You MUST tackle your own shortcomings before you can begin your new lifestyle. A healthy body is a healthy mind. Most importantly, for the topic of this book, a healthy mind means you can begin to speed-learn and become successful at it.

To help you get started, here are a few basic lifestyle habits you need to look at:

Time Management

Any improvements in your lifestyle goals will be based on the solid foundation of organized time management. Dissect a week in your typical routine of life, only then can you see where the shortfalls are.☐

For the first week, write down everything you do every hour. Make a chart that covers all seven days and all 24-hours. ☐

What is it that you're looking for?

At the end of the week when you assess your chart, you will be identifying:

- Gaps where you can introduce short bursts of physical exercise. Even if it means only a short brisk walk, this is better than sitting at a desk or doing nothing.

- Write down everything that you eat because it is very true that you are what you eat and drink. Your digestive system is breaking your food down into the good, bad and downright ugly. It's now time to make sure that there is more "goodness" entering your body.

- Record the times you go to bed and what time you get up. Make a note of any times that you feel a need to get up during the night. Also, jot down what you do when you get up. Do you have a habit of nighttime snacks? Are you visiting the toilet? Are you having trouble sleeping? These are all the situations you are looking to identify.

- Jot down a few words about the moods you are feeling. You don't need to write detailed emotions, but you are looking to see what effects your mood swings. You could simply use a code, such as:□

H for Happy
D for Depressed
F for fed up

Add a few of your own for the in-between emotions.

This will help you recognize if stress or depression is a problem in your life.

The idea of this whole concept is to find all your weaknesses and bad habits. Once you know them, you can tackle them and change your whole life around.

What does this have to do with fast-track learning?

Everything!

You are beginning your self-discipline routine by going right back to the basics.

Dietary Assessment

There are so many different cultural recipes and ways of eating that I cannot cover all the various diets everywhere in the world. What is generally agreed upon is that we need to ingest healthy natural foods. To compliment this guideline, we need to eat less unhealthy processed foods. □

Food is like a fashion and goes through many fads. To enjoy a healthy diet, you need to ignore the fads and follow your own knowledge and common sense. Most of us know the sensible options, but choose to ignore the obvious. Don't eat too much junk food. This covers take-outs, fast food, processed foods, and sugary foods. □

Not only will such foods increase your weight, but they will fog your brain instead of enhancing it. This is not a book about dietary needs, but high carb foods will cause your body to produce the wrong hormones. With stored up fats, you will gain weight, leading to that terrible feeling of lethargy. This is the road to ill health.□

Make some ground rules for yourself with regards to your dietary intake, such as:

- Stick to three meals a day and try NOT to snack between. Breakfast can be a quick healthy smoothie. Lunch should be made at home and not shop bought. Make sure your last meal has digested long before you go to bed.

- If you don't know how to home cook, then learn. Using your own ingredients is far healthier than shop bought meals. They can be full of hidden sugars and salt. Take lunch to work with you, so a take-out does not tempt you. You'll also save money by making your own meals.☐

- You must eat plenty of vegetables. Call them your brain food, and the darker they are, the more vitamins they contain. Eat fruit too, such as lots of berries that don't contain high concentrates of natural glucose sugars.

- Cut down on your meat intake, not only for your own health but for the environment too. Most specifically red meat. Meat has lots of protein, which is great brain food, but you can also get protein in many other healthy foods.☐

- Contrary to recent fads, not all fat is bad for you. It's making sure you are eating the right type of fats. You do not need to avoid foods with fats, just learn your good fats from your bad ones. Cook with olive oil. Avoid excess animal fats, including too much dairy products. Don't drink sugary drinks such as sodas and hot chocolate.☐

- As with sugar and carbohydrates, keep your alcohol and caffeine intake low.

These are but a few tips on healthy eating. Do your research and understand the food you are putting into your body. It is believed that a Mediterranean diet can feed the brain and keep you healthy.

Exercise

Latest figures claim that only 28% of Americans meet the recommended National Physical Activity Guide. With such reports, the chances are that you are guilty of not exercising your body enough.

You don't need to dash out and join an expensive gym. With a little imagination, it can cost nothing to keep your body fit. Your new regime should include the minimum recommendation. That is 150-minutes of moderate exercise, plus 75-minutes of vigorous exercise. It only amounts to under 4-hours per week. This is achievable for most people.

This is where the diary of your weekly agenda will be useful. Please note, this is not about losing weight because exercise alone will not achieve that. This is about the least amount of exercise you should be doing for your heart, muscles, and joints. Anything less is a health risk to your body.☐

If you could incorporate at least 5 x 30-minute walks into your week, you've already covered the 150-minutes. The 75-minute needs to get your heart pumping. Add another 2 x 35-minute very brisk walks to your weekly schedule, and you've done it. That's how easy it can be. Of course, it would be better if you could do more. It would also be better if you made the 75-minutes into something a little more vigorous for your muscles. Something that will tax your body a little more.☐

Sleep

By making these great improvements to your health, you should find that you sleep better too. Quality sleep is as important as good food and exercise. If you see that you're not getting the recommended 6-8-hours sleep, then you need to investigate what's bothering you. ☐

Stress-related worries can keep us all awake at night. If this sounds familiar to you, then you must not let these problems linger on for too long. Your new lifestyle covers many areas of your health. Consider your sleeping pattern as your personal battery charger. If it's not working properly, it needs fixing.☐

State of Mind

This follows on from the topic of Sleeping quite well because if you're not relaxed at the end of your day, your state of mind will not be in a healthy place. Most of us have stress in our lives, and it's not something that is easy to avoid. Instead, you need to learn how to do deal with it. If you ignore it, you are taking a risk with your health and may become ill. Your mental health is just as important as your physical health, so be proactive and take care of your mind. ☐

Learn some relaxation techniques for those moments when you get to wind down after a busy day. I know I said the brain is an amazing organ, but you still need to take care of it. Dealing with problems is much healthier than ignoring them. Do yourself a favor and look to resolve any of life's problems head-on. Your mind can function to its fullest potential as long as you're not bogged down with negative thoughts.☐

Relaxation Exercises

Some refer to these exercises as meditation because it means you can reflect upon your inner thoughts. It is a positive move to concentrate on your inner wellbeing. Such exercises can get you closer to understanding yourself.

Learn simple breathing techniques that you can do anywhere, anytime, such as the "4-7-8."

- Close your eyes and mouth.

- Take a deep breath through your nose, while you count to 4.

- Allow the intake of air to push out your stomach and lift your chest.

- Hold the breath and count to 7.

- Exhale the air out of an open mouth, while you count to 8.

- As you are repeating this exercise for a few minutes, clear your mind of what's going on around you. Visualize a sandy shore of the warm sun on your face.

- Repeat until your mind feels clear.

This is an exercise you can perform whenever you need a quick break from a busy schedule. Do it on a bus, in a tube, sat at your desk, in the toilet. It can be a lifesaver if you are feeling stressed. When you come out of the exercise, you should feel ready to face the world for a short while.

Added to this, you could also learn how to relax muscles throughout your body. It's good if you can lay down and work your way through your body from head to toe. If not, then focus on only a few muscles at a time.

- Start by concentrating on your feet and wiggle your toes. Clench any muscles you can feel in the foot and squeeze for around 5 seconds before you relax. Move your ankles around in circles.

- Make your way up your body. Next, do the squeezing in your calf muscles. Going on to the thigh, bottom, stomach chest, biceps, lower arm, fingers, hands and wrist, shoulders and neck. Finish off with the facial area.

- Pull distorted faces to get those facial muscles tense. Once you squeezed them for around 5 seconds, and then relax.

You'll be amazed how refreshed your body feels after you've completed this exercise. If you don't have the time to lay down, try doing it on and off throughout your day when you're sitting down. Work your way through your body muscles, but concentrating on only one part of the body whenever you have a moment to spare.

These are some simple techniques to set about improving your present lifestyle. Get yourself into peak condition. Once you have a healthy regime, it's time to begin your speed learning practices.

Chapter 3: Building Good Habits to Boost Your Memory

Sharpening Your Memory

Once you've organized your daily routine, you are ready to begin changing your life even further. These following recommendations are tried and tested and can help everyone, whether you are a:

- Student

- Parent

- Work full or part-time

- Company Director

- Retired

- Interested in improving your mind.

This is a guide meant for anyone who wishes to be successful in their life. All you must learn to do is use the tools of your own abilities. No financial investment is necessary, only the investment of your time.

Changes you should already have started to include in your life:

- Home cooked food
- Eliminating, or at least heavily reducing, sugars, carbs, and processed foods.
- Achieving, at the very least, the basic recommended weekly exercises.
- As a plus, if you have achieved all the above, your sleeping pattern should be much healthier.
- Finally, if stress begins to creep into your life, you should practice relaxation exercise. Breathing techniques should become a part of your life as should relaxing your muscles as I have shown you in chapter 2.

What is Memory?

The next step in achieving your goals towards accelerated learning is to improve your memory. Anyone with the right mindset and determination can improve their memory. Even those who use excuses, such as:

- "My memory is poor; it'll never improve."

- "I'm too old."

- "I'm too busy."

- "I can't be bothered."

- "It's all a load of rubbish."

- "I'm not clever enough."

Guess what - "I'm happy to announce to you that all the above are indeed nothing but poor excuses!"□

There is no reason why you cannot improve your memory, no matter your age or career choices. Whilst you can never achieve a photographic memory, there is much you can do to improve your day to day recall. By following our memory techniques, you will achieve the ability to focus. This will lead on to becoming more successful in your career, and in your general wellbeing.

Let's return to that powerful organ, the brain. Even more specifically, those neurons we discussed earlier. They are the brain cells and nerves that make up your brains communication network. The activity of those neurons transmits all the information that you see, smell, feel and learn in your everyday life.

Your brain decides if the new information you have absorbed is worth keeping or not. If it's worth keeping, it is then stored in your long term memory. Otherwise, it's only stored in the short term memory. Short term means it is information to be discarded and forgotten when you no longer needed.

The memories the brain stored in the long term memory banks can be recalled if needed again. By following the same pathway of neurons used to store the memory, the information can be called back out again. This storage system doesn't work as a photograph, capturing every detail. Sometimes when a memory is recalled, it may have become a little distorted or fuzzy. That's why you cannot totally rely on memory.

Age can weaken those neurons, and hence the system doesn't always work as well as it used to. This can be repaired though because the brain is one big muscle. It's up to you to make it stronger so it will work more efficiently. □

One of the most important processes in learning new information is your memory. If you don't learn how to utilize the memory to its full potential, then it's pointless learning new things. The brain will simply assume it is useless information and only store it in the short term memory. If though, you have good memory recall, you could potentially learn a wide range of new skills. For this reason, it's important to improve your memory skills. Only then can you begin to consider accelerated learning as an exciting way forward. By developing your memory skills, you are exercising your brain to be more efficient. Exercises such as these will extend your neuron pathways. Only then can you store more knowledge, making your mind much sharper. □

Mnemonics

The name of the Goddess of Memory in ancient Greek was Mnemosyne, meaning "remembrance." The ancient Greek word "mnemoniks," means "related to memory." These words have developed into the modern term of mnemonics, which is the study of improving our memory.

Mnemonics are a way of associating cues, images, sounds or abbreviations to help us remember large pieces of information. Here are some common mnemonics that most may be familiar with:

- "I" before "e" except after "c." Of course, this is not 100% proof, but it's a good rule of thumb for spellings.

- Here's a good way of remembering the same word spelled two-ways but has two different meanings. "A "principal" in a school is your PAL." Whereas, a "principle" that is something you believe in, is a rule."

- A way to remember where the points are on a compass is to spell out the word "NEWS" in an "S" shape. N (North) placed at the top. E (East) placed on the left. W (West) placed on the right and opposite E. Finishing with S (South) at the bottom.

As you can see, these aren't foolproof. As well as using the common ones, you can make your own up so you can remember things better.

Billy always spelled the word "restaurant" incorrect. He wrote it down as "restarAUNT." His problem was that he confused the ending with the two ways of spelling "aunt" and "ant." It was just one of those words that confused him, as can happen to us all. To remember the right type of "aunt," or "ant," at the end of the word, he told himself that whenever he thought of eating out, he would relate it to a bug. From then onwards he knew the ending of the word was spelled as "ANT."

Mnemonics can have a broad spectrum in covering ways of association. It has proven to be successful in memory recall. You may, though, have to remember an entire poem just so you can recall something factual, such as the days of the month:

> 30 days hath September, April, June, and November
> All the rest have 31 except for February alone.
> That has 28 with an extra one in a leap year.

It's the sort of rhyme you learn as a child and carry it through to adulthood. Many adults continue to use it to recall how many days there are in a month.

Mnemonics can be much more complex than these simple examples. You can even use images, such as in this biology question you might get in an exam paper:

- Question: Name 3 depressant drugs.

- Answer: Barbiturates, Alcohol, and Tranquilizers, whereby the initials spell BAT. If you had this question in an exam, you could remind yourself to visualize a bat.

You can create mnemonics in many forms:

- Patterns of letters such as acronyms

- Short phrases

- Images

- Numbers

- Poems

- Charts

- Songs

Do you remember the ABC song you might have sung as a child so you could learn the alphabet? It is a process that can be used at any age. By learning the order of a short phrase, that phrase can then lead on to recalling the order of the planets. There's even an entire song to help you recall all 50 states in the USA. What a powerful tool Mnemonics can be.

Loci Memory Palace

There is an alternative and effective mnemonic technique to enhance your memory. It is also one of the oldest memory techniques known as the Loci Method. Some may know it as a Memory Palace, Mind Palace or even the Memory Journey. It's believed to have originated from the Roman Empire and is sometimes known as the Roman Room technique. The method uses only one room and the items within that room. Loci is a Latin word meaning "Places." That is exactly what you need when you choose to use this method. For the Loci method to be successful, you will use a familiar place that you know, such as your own home. You can use any building as long as you know the layout.

To begin the Loci technique, you must imagine every aspect of your chosen location. That means the layout of the building and things such as furniture, ornaments, and pictures on the walls. This is important because each item is linked mentally to the facts you want to remember. Let's take you through a Mind Palace Journey:

- The idea is to associate something you need to memorize with a part of the building you have chosen.

- Walk through the front door, associate the first memory you want to recall with the door. Though its' not enough to simply associate the memory item with the door. Expand on this and visualize something unusual with the memory and the door. For example, if you need to remember a regular time for a train journey, then visualize a speeding train crashing through that particular door. Be imaginative as you go around your "place" associating memories with items. The more extreme the vision in your mind, the more likely you are to remember it. After all, don't we all remember the bad memories and never the good ones? ☐

- Going on, as you step through the door, visualize the hallway. It may have a mirror and coat hooks in particular places.

- Associate more facts with each picture and each piece of furniture as you walk through rooms. You can have each room for a particular theme of memories. This is great if you're studying different subjects.

It is quite hard work and tiring and does take some time to build up your memory palace. Deep concentration implants the memory association. Then further concentration is needed to recall the information throughout your memory palace. Don't expect this to happen in a day.

It does take practice but believes in your ability to do it because it has been proven to work. Clemens Mayer won the World Memory Championship in 2006, by using a Loci Memory Palace. He had 300 stop points in a journey throughout his own home. Each stop point was a memory he needed to recall.

If you manage to get the hang of it and it works for you, there is no reason why you can't have more than one "place." Each place can consist of different sets of facts that you need to memorize. Imagine the potential for your career; it is truly mind-boggling how far you could take this method. ☐

Chapter 4: How Does Speed Reading Target Your Goals?

The Art of Reading

Humans seem to have an inherent sense of always wanting to improve things. The discovery of the wheel made huge changes for mankind, from grinding flour to transportation. Where would we be today without the simplicity of the wheel? But it still took human knowledge to take this discovery forward.

In today's society, it can sometimes seem like the adage of every man for himself rings true. There's no doubting that we're expected to work hard if we want to live a quality life and knowledge alone is not enough. On top of that, we need the confidence to drive that knowledge forward.

- Speed reading will give you knowledge.
- Self-improvement will give you confidence.

Through self-improvement, you will become more aware of your "sense of self." Only then can you learn to create new opportunities so that "self" can grow. That's why humans are capable of such greatness.

By improving your lifestyle, you will open doorways that were previously locked. There is an immense amount of knowledge that has been handed down through generations. Feed that passion that drives us, and allow it to take you places you have not yet reached.

Whilst you can never know everything, you can begin to grasp some of it. The way to do that is to read the knowledge recorded in words. There exists so much reading matter in our world that a lifetime is not enough to get through it all. This is where the art of speed reading could be your way to tap into that vast store of available knowledge. Speed read.

Speed Read and Learn More

When you read for the purpose of learning, many advise reading the words slowly, at around 100-200 words per minute (wpm). This speed is even slower than reading a novel, which on the average is around 200-400 wpm. Yet, with speed reading, you can reach up to 700 wpm. Plus, if you do it right, you will also be learning.

The secret of speed reading is not how quickly you get through the text, but the quality of the words that you read. With speed reading, you will learn to pull out the important words and bypass the in-between words. That's how you'll find the ability to trawl through so much so fast because it's not necessary to read every word in the text.

Body Movements when Reading

To learn to speed read, there are a few bad practices that you will need to tackle right from the onset. These are probably habits you were not even aware you had:

Talking to Yourself

Like most people, the chances are that sometime during a long reading session, you will say the words as you read them. This might happen silently in your head, or even out loud. It might even be something you intentionally choose to do when you are studying. Believing that you may remember more facts if you say them out loud or in your head. The problem with this method of reading is that you will read slow as you plow through every single word. Your brain is actually working harder to activate neural pathways so you can do this task. The physical actions, such as muscle movement, listening and the use of your voice, are all using up more energy that is being wasted. All these actions slow you down, and you can only learn a small amount using this method. Stop saying words in your head or out loud. Of course, you need to register words in your mind, but you don't need to focus on any single word for too long.

Re-reading

How many times do you re-read a sentence because of background distraction? Or, you don't understand the word? It's almost like a compulsive disorder (OCD) as you keep reading it over and over again. This habit will get you nowhere fast. Once you begin to speed read, this compulsion should disappear.

Eye Movements

I could write a whole book on this topic alone as it is so extensive. It seems obvious to state that the eyes are the key tool for focusing on words, but they do much more than that. The eyes don't only move linearly across the page; they are also making rapid movements that are constantly broken up with stops. The fewer words you read, the less the eye muscles have to work, and then you won't get that dreaded tired eye syndrome. Eye movement will play an important role in speed reading. You will learn not only to reduce the eye movement but also to cut out the peripheral vision, so you're not distracted in any way.

Vocabulary

They say that the more you read, the wider your vocabulary becomes. With speed reading, that is, even more, the case.

It's a chicken and egg scenario. Read more, learn more words, and having a bigger vocabulary helps to speed your reading up. Speed reading means you CAN read more and so it goes on. The more words you have in your subconscious, the faster you can process information. You will find yourself pausing less due to unfamiliar words, because of your increased depth of vocabulary. □

Without a doubt, reading is a key skill for learning new topics. As you increase your knowledge, it can lead to new skills and improve your life chances. Does it not then make sense that speed reading will improve those chances even better? Once you have the ability to speed read, you are more likely to read text outside your usual reading materials and comfort zone. When you get to that stage, you are on your way to improving your career prospects. You will become a more engaged individual.□

Skim Reading

Many of us already use skim read when we want to read something that's not very interesting. Both skim and speed reading use rapid eye movements. The brain, though, is reacting differently to each of these reading techniques.

When skim reading, you are only getting an overview of the text, and not picking up any specific information. The brain isn't taxed in any way because if you see a word you don't understand, you can ignore it. The same goes for complicated sentences. You are not learning much because you are not processing large pieces of information □

When speed reading, or scanning, you are still learning. As you learn the techniques, it will allow you to pull out facts and figures. You will be grasping information and still learning new words. □

Stop   skim   reading   and   learn   how   to   scan   read   (speed   read)   instead.

Chapter 5: How to Start Speed Reading

Benefits of Reading

Reading can do more than entertaining the brain. Research by Thomas Corley, shows that 85% of self-made millionaires read at least 2 books a month? Note though, they don't read for entertainment or pleasure but for learning and education. Successful people are always taking on new knowledge, and that's how they got to be so prosperous and successful in the first place.

- Consider Benjamin Franklin, as far back as the 18th century. As a scientist, he invented some amazing life changing products from bifocals to a lightning rod. Not only was he one of the founding fathers to draft out the Declaration of Independence for the US, but he also went on to become the first postmaster general. He was indeed an avid reader and author.

The rich and famous reading habits don't stop there:

- Bill Gates reads around 50 books in a year. Enjoying nonfiction the most because it means he can constantly learn about the world. He likes to take notes when he comes across something new. His advice is, *to treat reading as an intellectual process to increase your mental capacity*. Even today, he blocks out at least one hour a day for a major reading session, and not newspapers but books. Books that allow your mind to actively learn new information, every day of your life.

- Mark Zuckerberg enjoys at least a couple of books every month.

- Elon Musk read 2 books a day as he grew up.

If you don't already do it, then you must begin to read every day.

Start today and continue with this habit.

You don't need to read for entertainment, though it does give a great deal of pleasure. It's the other benefits of reading that are essential. By varying your reading material, you can actively learn. Not everything you read will be truthful facts, particularly if you only target media publications. To give yourself a balanced view of the world, you should vary the type of reading material you are about to master.

Start by reading a few pages from a novel before you go to sleep at night. You could even have more than one novel on the go, swapping the genre with your mood. Find a nonfiction topic in life that has always interested you, but you never had time to pursue. It could be science, nature, gardening, or even the universe. Find a book on that topic and read it through on a daily basis.

Your vocabulary will be growing, and your memory will sharpen as your writing skills improve. You have now introduced a new entertainment option in your life. You have now joined the majority of people who enjoy reading, including those self-made millionaires. ☐

Once you are a regular reader, it's time to step up a notch and learn how to speed read. This is a method of soaking up even huge pieces of knowledge and doing it at a quick pace.

Benefits of Speed Reading

Imagine the potential of processing knowledge quicker. Perhaps you're a student who needs to cram lots of information into your brain for exams, or someone who sifts through reams of paperwork in their job. Speed reading enables the reader to work through their workload much quicker and with more efficiency.

Not that there is any shame in being a slow reader. Anyone who reads regularly should be proud of that fact. Slower readers will not process information as quickly as a speed reader. All it takes is learning the speed reading techniques. It is a skill that will help you realize how easy it is to increase your knowledge rapidly. It's not that you have more time on your hands; it's that you will train your brain to process information quicker.

It isn't the number of words that your eyes focus on as you read, but the quality of the words that you learn to pull out. Once you start practicing speed reading, you begin to miss out unimportant words. The secret to speed reading success is knowing which words to miss out and which words to focus on. At the same time, you still need to comprehend and understand the meaning of the words you are reading. If you're not learning, then it would be a wasted skill.☐

You are about to become a skilled reader simply by increasing your knowledge of the written language. You won't be sitting for any exams to prove your new skills. Through the vast exposure to the written words, your brain will start to recognize the new linguistic structure on the pages, almost to the point of predicting what's to follow, before you even get there. ☐

Learning new skills is best achieved by exposing your mind to things you don't already know. That's exactly what you will be doing when you start to read different styles of text. For example, the words of a novel are not be structured in the same way to the words of a scientific paper. The more you know about linguistics, the faster you will be able to plow through the many different structures of the written word.

The First Steps of Speed Reading

One of the first and most important skills you need so you can achieve good reading speeds is "focus." Your brain will soak information so quickly that if your mind wanders as you speed read, all the words you read will be forgotten. "Focus" is your new buzz word because without it you will not achieve the true skill of power reading.

For most of us, when we learned to read at a young age, we read every single word on a page. We were encouraged to run our fingers along the line of text as we read the words at a snail's pace. As an adult, you no longer need to read at such a slow pace. By speed reading, you whizz through reading material covering masses of information. It's all about cutting out chunks of words. If you have a cell phone, you most likely send out texts that have many abbreviated words in a sentence. Already you have learned the skill to communicate without using every necessary word in a sentence structure. □

Grammar is still vital when it comes to writing, but when reading, you can hop, skip and jump through sentences, paragraphs, and pages. □

It means learning how to pick out specific words in a sentence and ignoring all the other words. Our sentence example below has 11 words in total. Yet, to understand what is being described in the sentence, you only need to read 5 words. □

Here is the full sentence:

Sentence Example: There was once an old man who wore a big hat.□

When speed reading you need to capture the meaning of a sentence, without having to read every word. In the sentence below, if you only read the words with capital letters, can you comprehend the sentence?

- Sentence Example: There was once a MAN who wore a HAT.

Two words are not enough to understand the meaning of this sentence. We have pulled out the common nouns, which are the subject matter of the sentence. But, you only know it's about a "man" and a "hat." You could still interpret this sentence incorrectly, such as:

- Interpreted Sentences: "A young man lost his hat," or, "a giant man sat on his hat."

By reading too few words, you will not understand the substance of the sentence. Let's continue adding words to see how many we need to understand it. How do our 2 keywords attach together better? Now we need to capture the descriptive words, which are known as adjectives.□

In this sentence example, these words are, "old" and "big." This means we must now read 4 words: □

- Sentence Example: There was once an OLD MAN who wore a BIG HAT.

We do still not comprehend the meaning of the sentence, but we're almost there. We still need one more connecting word, which is the verb, or the doing word. In this instance it is the word, "wore."

Does our sentence make sense with 5 words?

- Sentence Example: There was once an OLD MAN who WORE a BIG HAT.

By reading only, "Old man wore big hat," we can comprehend the meaning of the example sentence. We skipped six words when we read this sentence. It is not the speed of the reading, but knowing which words to ignore.☐

You don't need to know what a noun, adjective or verb is, the chances are that your brain is already wired to pick out those keywords. I only used the technical term to describe how you can cut an 11-word sentence down to a 5-word sentence.

At this level, this type of reading still resembles the technique called skim reading. Now, you need to learn other techniques to further your skill of speed reading.

Chapter 6 Speed Reading Techniques

Learning how to sprint through text is not a skill you can learn overnight. You need to commit to practice sessions as with any new skill.

Groups of Words

Normally, as you read, the focus of your eyes takes in a word at a time. To speed this up, you need to train your eyes to take in groups of words. Start with around 3 words.

Exercise 1:

Take any book and practice jumping along the text by focusing on 3 words at a time. In your mind, pick out a few words as you do so. In the beginning, it doesn't matter which words you pick out. You're simply practicing the technique of jumping through a line of text in 3-word blocks.

To begin with, it might seem like you've read a jumbled up incoherent mess. At this stage, it doesn't matter. It is the same as a runner would practice at a warm up. By using this technique, you will become more proficient at speed-reading. In time, you will find that your eyes and brain focus on what it considers to be the important words. The other words are ignored as in our sentence example in chapter 5.

Meta Guiding

Now that you are reading words in groups across the page, let's move to a method of guiding you down the page. This is meta guiding, also known as the pointer method or even hand pacing. They are all attempting to do the same thing, guide you down the page.

Exercise 2:

You are going to need a piece of card or a ruler. When you were very young and started to learn to read, you may have used your finger to guide you through each word as you read it out loud. Don't use your finger just yet as you need to block off the following lines to practice this technique. By blocking off what is coming further down the page, your eyes will focus better on what you are reading.

Continue to read words in groups, but place your card under the line you are reading. You will need to move the card at speed as you come to each line. It will seem a little clumsy at first, but you are training your eyes to concentrate on the line that is being read.

Once the card, or ruler, is slowing you down, change your marker to your finger, or a pen with a lid on so you don't mark the text.

Once you master these two techniques, you will be:

- Skipping words
- Reading groups of words rather than individual words
- Scan reading much quicker

Practice these techniques with easier reading material, such as nonfiction or magazine articles.

Highlighting

It's time to make notes of what you're actually reading.

Exercise 3:

There will come a time when you no longer need a marker. When you get to that point, you can start to jot down the words that your eyes pick up. Initially, it might slow down your reading again, but it will move you on to the next stage. The notes don't need to make sense at this stage because you are still learning the technique.

Have a quick look at what you've written. Do your words make sense? If they do, then you have comprehended the text in this new method of reading. If they don't, then you need to keep practicing.

This is pre-reading text, and you can do this for the whole chapters. The notes you take will give you an idea if you want to go back and get more information. If you do, you can re-read only the parts that matter, and miss out the parts of the book that are of no use to you.

As you can see, it's not so much about reading all the words at a fast speed. It's more about getting through the text at speed to pull out a few important words. Then you can identify where in the book you need to focus when you re-read. This is not the same as the bad habit of re-reading a word, sentence or paragraph over and over. This is about learning whereabouts in an entire book and lays the important information.

You may also find that by reading the headings, it helps you to skip through a book at speed.

Such reading tips accumulate together to help you pick up the experience of speed reading.

Benchmarking your new skill

So that you can see your progress whilst you train to speed read, you need to set up a simple form of benchmarking. This will help you analyze your own progress.

It does not need to be a complicated process. It can be as simple as timing yourself with the same exercise each day. If your progression slows down or even comes to a stop, then challenge yourself to a more difficult exercise.

If this happens, you can be confident that you are progressing with your speed reading skills.

5 Tips for the Discipline of Learning New Skill Sets

Daily practice

This is essential if you are not to let slip any of the progress you have made. All that brain exercise as you practice alters the chemistry of your body. The neural pathways in your brain will develop and multiply; hence your brain is now improving. Once you're over the initial hurdle of kickstarting the growth of new brain cells, you will never look back. It's not easy, but it will be worth it.

Everyday habits

Your new habits should start to include your new skill sets. They should become a part of your life in a natural way. Studies are showing that by keeping your brain active, it is a way of reducing the risk of dementia.

Challenge your skill levels

You should always seek to improve on your present limitations. Don't allow any skills to become passive. By improving on the skill set of speed reading, you do not only improve your speed reading skills but your general knowledge too. This will help you feel more confident and content with life. It will be hard work, but the new you will be reaping the rewards of an upwardly mobile career path or a simple feeling of amazing self-satisfaction.

Reap Rewards

All your hard work should be paying off, as areas of your new lifestyle improve. Speed reading improves your reading skills and opens up the opportunity of a progressive lifestyle. You can now look forward to:

- A promotion in your career.

- Improved health as you better understand the need for a healthy lifestyle.

- You will gain enhanced feelings of contentment and personal satisfaction, and any negative feelings you had in the past will be banished from your life. You may even seek to help others resolve their problems as you come out of your cocoon and use your new knowledge to explore the world.

<u>Take care of yourself.</u> □

In this life, it is ultra important that you take care of yourself. Never forget how important you are to yourself. It is not selfish to look after your own body and mind; it is common sense. You will do more good in the world with a healthy balanced mind than you did before you opened up your life to self-improvement.□

Conclusion

Intelligence can be measured in many ways. We've all heard of an IQ test, but how accurate is this to your understanding of life? Have you ever practiced at it and noticed that you could improve on the results? Psychologist, Howard Gardner, believes that the IQ test only focuses on logical and linguistic skills. Further, he states that there are many other components to measuring a person's intelligence. http://www.aboutintelligence.co.uk/what-intelligence.html

What about your personal EQ results? This is a modern definition and includes your Emotional intelligence. After all, this is what separates any form of AI from human intelligence. Emotions are complex, and their triggers vary. It would be almost impossible ever to create an AI that possessed true emotional intelligence. Emotions separate us humans from animals. They are the key to our very existence.☐

Challenging your lifestyle can lead to becoming more pragmatically intelligent. It can also help to increase your IQ level. Multitasking your life away can only slow down your progress. This is because you lack "focus." The need to focus and develop is an important one. Don't be afraid of questioning the facts around you. It will help you to grow in your "intelligence."☐

- Did you ever think it is possible that speed reading was a skill you could learn without a teacher? ☐

- The good news is that it is a skill that anyone can achieve, and that means you too.

Follow the instructions in this guide, and you will soon be sprinting through books, AND comprehending contents. More knowledge opens up new pathways to learning a huge variety of skills. ☐

Never be afraid of the experts. They are knowledgeable in their particular fields. They have taken the time to learn their skill and will be rich in information. ☐

Always invite new information into your mind, assess it and enhance upon it. Expand your view of the world by using that wonderful organ called the brain. Not only will you be a more focused individual, but it will open many doors of opportunity.

This cannot happen unless you take care of the "self." That is the key starting point, and the rest will follow. Be brave and challenge your present lifestyle. Force changes for the better so you can reap the rewards. By learning new skills that you thought were out of your reach, you are developing your "self." This is a richness that money cannot buy.